TAX LAW
Essential Legal Terms Explained You Need To Know About Tax Law!

DR. PETER JOHNSON

Copyright © 2019

All rights reserved.

ISBN: 9781799098638

TEXT COPYRIGHT © [DR. PETER JOHNSON]

all rights reserved. No part of this guide may be reproduced in any form without permission in writing from the publisher except in the case of brief quotations embodied in critical articles or reviews.

Legal & disclaimer

The information contained in this book and its contents is not designed to replace or take the place of any form of medical or professional advice; and is not meant to replace the need for independent medical, financial, legal or other professional advice or services, as may be required. The content and information in this book have been provided for educational and entertainment purposes only.

The content and information contained in this book have been compiled from sources deemed reliable, and it is accurate to the best of the author's knowledge, information, and belief. However, the author cannot guarantee its accuracy and validity and cannot be held liable for any errors and/or omissions. Further, changes are periodically made to this book as and when needed. Where appropriate and/or necessary, you must consult a professional (including but not limited to your doctor, attorney, financial advisor or such other professional advisor) before using any of the suggested remedies, techniques, or information in this book.

Upon using the contents and information contained in this book, you agree to hold harmless the author from and against any damages, costs, and expenses, including any legal fees potentially resulting from the application of any of the information provided by this book. This disclaimer applies to any loss, damages or injury caused by the use and application, whether directly or indirectly, of any advice or information presented, whether for breach of contract, tort, negligence, personal injury, criminal intent, or under any other cause of action.

You agree to accept all risks of using the information presented inside this book.

You agree that by continuing to read this book, where appropriate and/or necessary, you shall consult a professional (including but not limited to your doctor, attorney, or financial advisor or such other advisor as needed) before using any of the suggested remedies, techniques, or information in this book.

Table of Contents

Introduction 6

Law On Personal Income Tax 7

    General Provisions 7

    Taxable Incomes 8

    Tax-Exempt Incomes 11

    Tax Reduction 13

    Tax Period 14

    Tax Administration And Tax Refund 15

    Taxable Incomes From Business 16

    Taxable Incomes From Salaries Or Wages 18

    Taxable Incomes From Capital Investment 19

    Taxable Incomes From Capital Transfer 20

    Taxable Incomes From Real Estate Transfer 21

    Taxable Incomes From Copyright 22

    Taxable Incomes From Commercial Franchising ... 23

    Taxable Incomes From Inheritances Or Gifts 24

    Reduction For Charity Or Humanitarian Donations 25

    Responsibilities Of Income-Paying Organizations And Individuals And Responsibilities Of Resident Taxpayers 26

    Responsibilities Of Income-Paying Organizations And Individuals And Responsibilities Of Non-Resident Taxpayers 27

Law On Value-Added Tax 28

    General Provisions 28

    Tax Bases 29

Taxable Price 30

Tax Calculation Methods 32

Tax Credit Method 33

Method Of Calculation Of Tax Based Directly On Added Value 34

Law On Enterprise Income Tax 35

General Provisions 35

Taxable Incomes 36

Determination Of Taxed Income 37

Law On Excise Tax 38

General Provisions 38

Taxpayers 39

Tax Bases 40

Taxed Price 41

Law On Severance Tax 42

General Provisions 42

Severance Tax-Liable Objects 43

Severance Tax Payers 44

Severance Tax Bases 45

Natural Resource Output Used For Severance Tax Calculation .. 46

Severance Tax-Liable Prices 47

Law On Environmental Protection Tax 48

General Provisions 48

Interpretation Of Terms 49

Taxable Subject 50

- Taxpayer 52
- Tax Base 53
- Taxable Time 54
- Tax Declaration, Tax Calculation And Tax Payment 55

The Law On Export And Import Duties 56

- General Provisions 56
- Taxed Goods 57
- Taxpayers 58
- Taxable Value And Time For Tax Calculation 59
- Anti-Dumping Duties 60
- Countervailing Duties 61
- Tax Reduction 62
- Tax Refund 63

Conclusion 64

Check Out Other Books 65

Introduction

Thank you and congratulate you for downloading the book *"TAX LAW: Essential Legal Terms Explained You Need To Know About Tax Law!"*

With a clear, concise, and engaging writing style, Dr. Peter Johnson will help you with a practical understanding of tax law topics about *Law On Personal Income Tax, Law On Value-Added Tax, Law On Enterprise Income Tax, Law On Excise Tax, Law On Severance Tax, Law On Environmental Protection Tax, The Law On Export And Import Duties*; provide you a road map to navigating tax law rules and help you build a foundation for understanding the overall picture and **much much more**. This book delivers extensive coverage of every aspect of the law and details the duties a paralegal is expected to perform when working within tax law. High-level, comprehensive coverage is combined with cutting-edge developments and foundational concepts.

As the author of the book, I promise this book will be an invaluable source of legal reference for professionals, international lawyers, law students, business professionals and anyone else who want to improve their use of legal terminology, succinct clarification of legal terms and have a better understanding of types of tax law. This book provides you with a comprehensive and highly practical approach in legal contexts, the world of tax law. All legal terms and phrases are well written and explained clearly in plain English.

Thank you again for purchasing this book, and I hope you enjoy it.

Let's get started!

LAW ON PERSONAL INCOME TAX

GENERAL PROVISIONS

This Law provides for personal income taxpayers, taxable incomes, incomes eligible for personal income tax exemption or reduction, and personal income tax bases.

TAXABLE INCOMES

Incomes liable to personal income tax include the following kinds of income:

1. Incomes from business activities, including:

a/ Incomes from goods production or trading or service provision;

b/ Incomes from independent professional activities of individuals possessing practice licenses or certificates in accordance with law.

2. Incomes from salaries and wages, including:

a/ Salaries, wages and amounts of similar nature;

b/ Allowances, except for those paid under legal provisions on preferential treatment of persons with meritorious services; defense or security allowances; hazard or danger allowances for persons working in branches, occupations or jobs at places where exist hazardous or dangerous elements; allowances for attraction of laborers to work in certain branches or in certain regions specified by law; allowances for sudden difficulties, allowances for laborers having labor accident or suffering from occupational disease, lump-sum maternity or child adoption allowances; allowances for working capacity loss, lump-sum retirement allowances, monthly survivorship allowances, severance and job loss allowances, other allowances paid by the Social Insurance, and allowances for combat of social evils;

c/ Remuneration of all kinds;

d/ Sums of money earned for participation in business associations, boards of directors, control boards, management boards and other organizations;

e/ Other monetary or non-monetary benefits received by taxpayers;

f/ Bonuses, rewards, except for rewards accompanying honorary titles conferred by the State or international or national prizes; rewards for technical renovations, creations or inventions recognized by competent state agencies; rewards for detection and reporting of illegal acts to competent state agencies.

3. Incomes from capital investment, including:

a/ Interests;

b/ Dividends;

c/ Incomes from capital investment in other forms, except for government bond interests.

4. Incomes from capital transfer, including:

a/ Incomes from transfer of capital holdings in economic organizations;

b/ Incomes from transfer of securities;

c/ Incomes from transfer of capital in other forms.

5. Incomes from transfer of real estate, including:

a/ Incomes from transfer of rights to use land and assets attached to land;

b/ Incomes from transfer of right to own or use residential houses;

c/ Incomes from transfer of right to lease land or water surface;

d/ Other incomes earned from transfer of real estate.

6. Incomes from won prizes, including:

a/ Lottery winnings;

b/ Sales promotion winnings;

c/ Betting or casino winnings;

d/ Winnings in prized games and contests and other forms of winning.

7. Incomes from copyright, including:

a/ Incomes from assignment or licensing of intellectual property objects;

b/ Incomes from technology transfer.

8. Incomes from commercial franchising.

9. Incomes from inheritances that are securities, capital holdings in economic organizations or business establishments, real estate and other assets subject to ownership or use registration.

10. Incomes from gifts that are securities, capital holdings in economic organizations or business establishments, real estate and other assets subject to ownership or use registration.

TAX-EXEMPT INCOMES

1. Incomes from transfer of real estate between spouses; parents and their children; adoptive parents and their adopted children; fathers-in-law or mothers-in-law and daughters-in-law or sons-in-law; grandparents and their grandchildren; or among blood siblings.

2. Incomes from transfer of residential houses, rights to use residential land and assets attached to residential land received by individuals who have only one residential house or land plot each.

3. Incomes from the value of land use rights of individuals who are allocated land by the State.

4. Incomes from receipt of inheritances or gifts that are real estate between spouses, parents and their children; adoptive parents and their adopted children; fathers-in-law or mothers-in-law and daughters-in-law or sons-in-law; grandparents and their grandchildren; or among blood siblings.

5. Incomes of households and individuals directly engaged in agricultural or forest production, salt making, aquaculture, fishing and trading of aquatic resources not yet processed into other products or preliminarily processed aquatic products.

6. Incomes from conversion of agricultural land allocated by the State to households and individuals for production.

7. Incomes from interests on deposits at credit institutions or interests from life insurance policies.

8. Incomes from foreign exchange remittances.

9. Wages paid for night shift or overtime work, which are higher than those paid for day shifts or prescribed working hours in accordance with law.

10. Retirement pensions paid by the Social Insurance.

11. Incomes from scholarships, including:

a/ Scholarships granted from the state budget;

b/ Scholarships granted by domestic and foreign organizations under their study promotion programs.

12. Incomes from indemnities paid under life insurance policies, non-life insurance policies, compensations for labor accidents, compensations paid by the State and other compensations as provided for by law.

13. Incomes received from charity funds licensed or recognized by competent state agencies and operating for charity, humanitarian or non-profit purposes.

14. Incomes received from governmental or non-governmental foreign aid for charity or humanitarian purposes approved by competent state agencies.

TAX REDUCTION

Taxpayers who face difficulties caused by natural disasters, fires, accidents or severe diseases and affecting their tax payment ability may be considered for tax reduction corresponding to the extent of damage they suffer from but not exceeding payable tax amounts.

TAX PERIOD

1. For residents, tax period is specified as follows:

a/ Annual tax period, which is applicable to incomes from business, salaries and wages.

b/ Tax period upon each time of income generation, which is applicable to incomes from capital investment; incomes from capital transfer, except for incomes from securities transfer; incomes from real estate transfer; incomes from prizes; incomes from copyright; incomes from commercial franchising; incomes from inheritances; and gifts.

c/ Tax period upon each transfer or annual tax period, which is applicable to securities transfer. Individuals who apply the annual tax period shall register with tax offices at the beginning of the year.

2. For non-residents, the tax period counted upon each time of income generation is applicable to all their taxable incomes.

TAX ADMINISTRATION AND TAX REFUND

1. Tax registration, declaration, withholding, payment, finalization and refund, handling of violations of the tax law, and tax administration measures comply with legal provisions on tax administration.

2. Individuals are entitled to tax refund in the following cases:

a/ Their paid tax amounts are larger than payable tax amounts;

b/ They have paid tax but their taxed incomes do not reach a tax-liable level;

c/ Other cases decided by competent state agencies.

TAXABLE INCOMES FROM BUSINESS

1. A taxable income from business is determined to be equal to turnover minus reasonable expenses related to the generation of the taxable income from business in a tax period.

2. Turnover means the total of sales, processing remuneration, commissions, goods or service provision charges generated in a tax period from goods production and trading or service provision.

The time of determination of turnover is the time of transfer of ownership of goods or completion of services or the time of making goods sale or service provision invoices.

3. Reasonable expenses related to the generation of taxable incomes from business in a tax period include:

a/ Salaries, wages, remuneration and other payments to laborers;

b/ Expenses for raw materials, fuels, materials, energy and goods used for production or business, charges for services purchased from outside;

c/ Expenses for depreciation, regular repair and maintenance of fixed assets used for production or business;

d/ Paid interests;

e/ Management expenses;

f/ Taxes, charges and fees payable under law and allowed to be accounted as expenses;

g/ Other expenses related to the generation of incomes.

4. The determination of turnover and expenses is based on accounting norms, standards, regulations, documents and books prescribed by law.

5. If many persons jointly conduct business activities under the same business registration, taxable income of each of them is determined according to one of the following principles:

a/ In proportion to their capital contributions stated in the business registration;

b/ Under their agreement stated in the business registration;

c/ According to the average per-capita income in case the business registration neither states their capital contributions nor contains any agreement on income division among them.

6. For business individuals who fail to strictly comply with regulations on accounting, invoices and documents and cannot measure turnover, expenses and taxable income, competent tax offices shall predetermine turnover and the ratio of taxable income in order to determine taxable income suitable to each industry or business line under the law on tax administration.

TAXABLE INCOMES FROM SALARIES OR WAGES

1. A taxable income from salary or wage is determined to be equal to the total of incomes earned by a taxpayer in a tax period.

2. Time of determination of a taxable income from salary or wage is the time when an organization or individual pays income to a taxpayer or when a taxpayer receives income.

TAXABLE INCOMES FROM CAPITAL INVESTMENT

1. A taxable income from capital investment is the total of incomes from capital investment earned by a taxpayer in a tax period.

2. Time of determination of a taxable income from capital investment is the time when an organization or individual pays income to a taxpayer or when a taxpayer receives income.

TAXABLE INCOMES FROM CAPITAL TRANSFER

1. A taxable income from capital transfer is determined to be equal to the selling price minus the buying price and reasonable expenses related to the generation of income from capital transfer.

2. If the buying price and expenses related to the securities transfer are unidentifiable, taxable income is determined to be the selling price of securities.

3. Time of determination of a taxable income from capital transfer is the time when the capital transfer transaction is completed in accordance with law.

TAXABLE INCOMES FROM REAL ESTATE TRANSFER

1. A taxable income from real estate transfer is determined to be equal to the real estate transfer price upon the transfer minus the real estate buying price and related expenses, specifically as follows:

a/ Real estate transfer price is the contractual price at the time of transfer;

b/ Real estate buying price is the contractual price at the time of purchase;

c/ Related expenses to be subtracted are those recorded in vouchers and invoices lawfully, including charges and fees related to land use rights as prescribed by law; expenses for land revamp, house renovation, ground leveling; expenses for investment in building residential houses, infrastructures and architectures on land; and other expenses related to the real estate transfer.

2. If the buying price and expenses related to the transfer of a real estate are unidentifiable, the taxable income is determined to be the real estate transfer price.

3. Time of determination of a taxable income from real estate transfer is the time when the transfer contract becomes effective in accordance with law.

TAXABLE INCOMES FROM COPYRIGHT

1. A taxable income from copyright is an income earned by a taxpayer when assigning or licensing an intellectual property object or transferring a technology under a contract.

2. Time of determination of a taxable income from copyright is the time when an organization or individual pays income to a taxpayer.

TAXABLE INCOMES FROM COMMERCIAL FRANCHISING

1. A taxable income from commercial franchising is an income earned by a taxpayer under a commercial franchising contract.

2. Time of determination of a taxable from commercial franchising is the time when an organization or individual pays income to a taxpayer.

TAXABLE INCOMES FROM INHERITANCES OR GIFTS

1. A taxable income from inheritance or gift is the value of an inherited asset or a gift received by a taxpayer upon each time of inheritance or gift receipt.

2. Time of determination of a taxable income is specified as follows:

a/ For an income from inheritance, it is the time when a taxpayer receives an inherited estate;

b/ For an income from gift, it is the time when an organization or individual presents a gift to a taxpayer or when a taxpayer receives the income.

REDUCTION FOR CHARITY OR HUMANITARIAN DONATIONS

Charity or humanitarian donations are deductible from pre-tax income from business, salary or wage of a resident taxpayer, including:

a/ Donations to organizations or establishments that care for or nurture children in special plights, disabled people and supportless elderly people.

b/ Donations to charity funds, humanitarian funds or study promotion funds.

RESPONSIBILITIES OF INCOME-PAYING ORGANIZATIONS AND INDIVIDUALS AND RESPONSIBILITIES OF RESIDENT TAXPAYERS

1. Responsibility to make tax declaration, withholding, payment and finalization is specified as follows:

a/ Income-paying organizations and individuals shall make tax declaration, withhold and remit tax into the state budget, and make tax finalization for all kinds of taxable income they pay to taxpayers;

b/ Individuals who have taxable incomes shall make tax declaration, pay tax into the state budget and make tax finalization for all their incomes in accordance with the law on tax administration.

2. Income-paying organizations and individuals shall supply information on incomes and dependants of taxpayers under their management in accordance with law.

RESPONSIBILITIES OF INCOME-PAYING ORGANIZATIONS AND INDIVIDUALS AND RESPONSIBILITIES OF NON-RESIDENT TAXPAYERS

1. Income-paying organizations and individuals shall withhold and remit tax into the state budget upon each time of payment of taxable incomes to taxpayers.

2. Non-resident taxpayers shall make tax declaration and payment upon each time of generation of taxable income in accordance with the law on tax administration.

LAW ON VALUE-ADDED TAX

GENERAL PROVISIONS

This Law provides for objects subject and not subject to value-added tax, taxpayers, tax bases, tax calculation methods, and tax credit and refund.

TAX BASES

Value-added tax bases include taxable price and tax rate.

TAXABLE PRICE

1. The taxable price is specified as follows:

a/ For goods and services sold by business establishments, the taxable price is the selling price exclusive of value-added tax. For excise tax-liable goods and services, the taxable price is the selling price inclusive of excise tax but exclusive of value-added tax;

b/ For imported goods, the taxable price is the border-gate import price plus import tax (if any) and excise tax (if any). The border-gate import price shall be determined under regulations on prices for calculating import tax;

c/ For goods and services used for barter, internal consumption or donation, the taxable price is the price for calculating value-added tax on goods and services of the same or equivalent kinds at the time of barter, consumption or donation;

d/ For asset lease, the taxable price is the rent exclusive of value-added tax;

In case of asset lease for which rents are paid periodically or in advance for a certain lease duration, the taxable price is the rent paid periodically or in advance, exclusive of value-added tax;

In case of hiring foreign machinery, equipment or means of transport which cannot be manufactured at home for sublease, the taxable price excludes the rent payable to the foreign party;

e/ For goods sold by mode of installment or deferred payment, the taxable price is the lump-sum selling price of such goods, exclusive of value-added tax, excluding the interest on installment or deferred payment;

f/ For goods processing, the taxable price is the processing remuneration exclusive of value-added tax;

g/ For construction and installation activities, the taxable price is the value of the handed-over work, work item or job, exclusive of value-added tax. If construction or installation activities do not cover materials, machinery or equipment, the taxable price is the construction or installation value, excluding the value of materials, machinery or equipment;

h/ For real estate trading, the taxable price is the real estate-selling price exclusive of value-added tax, excluding the charge for transferring land use rights or the land rent remittable into the state budget;

i/ For commission-enjoying goods or service trading agency and brokerage, the taxable price is the commission on these activities, exclusive of value-added tax;

TAX CALCULATION METHODS

Value-added tax calculation methods include value-added tax credit method and method of calculation of tax based directly on added value.

TAX CREDIT METHOD

1. The value-added tax credit method is specified as follows:

a/ The payable value-added tax amount according to the tax credit method is the output value-added tax amount minus the creditable input value-added tax amount;

b/ The output value-added tax amount is the total amount of value-added tax on sold goods and services indicated in the added-value invoice;

2. The tax credit method applies to business establishments which fully observe regulations on accounting, invoices and documents as prescribed by the law on accounting, invoices and documents, and register to pay tax according to the tax credit method.

METHOD OF CALCULATION OF TAX BASED DIRECTLY ON ADDED VALUE

The method of calculation of tax based directly on added value is specified as follows:

a/ The payable value-added tax amount according to the method of calculation of tax based directly on added value is the added value of sold goods or services multiplied by the value-added tax rate;

b/ The added value is the selling price of goods or services minus the purchase price of such goods or services.

LAW ON ENTERPRISE INCOME TAX

GENERAL PROVISIONS

This Law provides for enterprise income taxpayers, taxable incomes, tax-exempt incomes, tax bases, tax calculation methods, and tax incentives.

TAXABLE INCOMES

1. Taxable incomes include income from goods and service production and business activities.

2. Other incomes cover income from the transfer of capital or real estate; income from the right to own or use assets; income from the transfer, lease or liquidation of assets; income from interests, loans or foreign currency sales; refund of provisions; recovery of bad debts already written off; collection of payable debts of unidentifiable creditors; omitted income from previous years business activities, and other incomes.

DETERMINATION OF TAXED INCOME

1. Taxed income in a tax period is the taxable income minus tax-exempt incomes and losses carried forward from previous years.

2. Taxable income is turnover minus deductible expenses for production and business activities plus other incomes.

3. Income from real estate transfer must be separately determined for tax declaration and payment.

LAW ON EXCISE TAX

GENERAL PROVISIONS

This Law provides for taxable and non-taxable objects, and payers, bases, refund, deduction and reduction of excise tax.

Taxable objects

1. Goods:

a/ Cigarettes, cigars and other tobacco preparations used for smoking, inhaling, chewing, sniffing or keeping in mouth;

b/ Liquor;

c/ Beer;

d/ Under-24 seat cars, including cars for both passenger and cargo transportation with two or more rows of seats and fixed partitions between passenger holds and cargo holds;

e/ Two- and three-wheeled motorcycles of a cylinder capacity of over 125 cm^3;

f/ Aircraft and yachts;

g/ Gasoline of all kinds, naphtha, reformade components and other components for mixing gasoline;

h/ Air-conditioners of 90,000 BTU or less;

i/ Playing cards;

j/ Votive gilt papers and votive objects.

2. Services:

a/ Dance halls;

b/ Massage parlors and karaoke bars;

c/ Casinos; prize-winning video games, including jackpot and slot games and games on similar machines;

d/ Betting;

e/ Golf business, including the sale of membership cards and golf playing tickets;

f/ Lottery business.

TAXPAYERS

Excise taxpayers include producers and importers of goods and providers of services which are subject to excise tax.

Exporters that purchase excise tax-liable goods from producers for export and do not export but sell them domestically shall pay excise tax.

TAX BASES

Excise tax bases include the taxed price of a taxable goods or service and the tax rate. The payable excise tax amount is the excise taxed price multiplied by the excise tax rate.

TAXED PRICE

The excise taxed price of a goods or service is the goods selling price or the service charge, exclusive of excise tax and value-added tax. Specifically:

1. For domestically produced goods, it is the selling price set by the producer;

2. For imported goods, it is the import-duty calculation price plus the import duty. For imported goods eligible for import duty exemption or reduction, it is exclusive of the exempted or reduced import duty amount;

3. For processed goods, it is the taxed price of the goods sold by processing-ordering establishment or the selling price of the product of the same or similar kind at the same time with the time of goods sale;

4. For goods sold on installment or deferred payment, it is the one-off selling price of such goods, exclusive of the installment or deferred payment interest;

5. For services, it is the service charge set by the service provider. The service provision in a number of cases is specified as follows:

a/ For golf business, it is the selling price of the membership card or golf-playing ticket, inclusive of the golf playing charge and deposit (if any);

b/ For casino, prize-winning video game and betting business, it is the turnover from such business minus the prize already paid to customers;

c/ For dance hall, massage parlor and karaoke bar business, it is the turnover from such business.

6. For goods and services used for barter, internal consumption or donation, it is the excise taxed price of the goods or service of the same or similar kind at the time of barter, internal consumption or donation.

LAW ON SEVERANCE TAX

GENERAL PROVISIONS

This Law provides for severance tax-liable objects, severance tax payers, severance tax bases, and severance tax declaration, payment, exemption and reduction.

SEVERANCE TAX-LIABLE OBJECTS

1. Metallic minerals.

2. Non-metallic minerals.

3. Crude oil.

4. Natural gas, coal gas.

5. Natural forest products, other than animals.

6. Natural aquatic products, including marine animals and plants.

7. Natural water, including surface water and groundwater.

8. Natural swallow's nests.

SEVERANCE TAX PAYERS

Severance tax payers include organizations and individuals that exploit severance tax-liable natural resources.

SEVERANCE TAX BASES

Severance tax bases include natural resource output used for severance tax calculation, severance tax-liable price and severance tax rate.

NATURAL RESOURCE OUTPUT USED FOR SEVERANCE TAX CALCULATION

1. For an exploited natural resource the quantity, weight or volume of which can be determined, the natural resource output used for royally calculation is the quantity, weight or volume of natural resource actually exploited in a severance tax period.

2. For an exploited natural resource the quantity, weight or volume of which cannot be determined because this natural resource contains different substances and impurities, the natural resource output used for severance tax calculation shall be determined based on the quantity, weight or volume of each substance obtained from sorting and classification.

3. For natural resources which are not sold but used for turning out other products, if their actually exploited quantity, weight or volume cannot be directly determined, the natural resource output used for severance tax calculation shall be determined based on the output of products turned out in a severance tax period and the use norm of natural resource per unit of product.

SEVERANCE TAX-LIABLE PRICES

The severance tax-liable price is the exploiter's selling price of a unit of natural resource product, exclusive of value-added tax.

LAW ON ENVIRONMENTAL PROTECTION TAX

GENERAL PROVISIONS

This Law provides for taxable subject, un-taxable subject, taxpayers, tax base, tax declaration, tax calculation, tax payment and environmental protection tax refund.

INTERPRETATION OF TERMS

In this Law, the terms below are construed as follows:

1. Environmental protection tax means indirect-collected tax, collected on products and goods (hereafter referred to as goods) when used to cause negative environmental impacts.

2. Absolute tax rate means tax rate prescribed by the amount of money per unit of taxable goods.

3. Taxable-plastic bag means bags; packages are made from polyethylene plastic film unit, its technical name is a porous plastic bag

4. Hydrogen-chlorofluorocarbon liquid (HCFC) means group of substance causing reduction of ozone used as refrigerant.

TAXABLE SUBJECT

1. Gasoline, oil, grease, including:

a) Gasoline, except ethanol;

b) aircraft fuel;

c) diesel oil;

d) Petroleum;

e) Fuel oil;

f) lubricants;

g) Grease.

2. Coal, including:

a) Lignite;

b) Anthracite Coal (anthracite);

c) Fat coal;

d) Other coal.

3. Hydrogen-chlorofluorocarbon liquid (HCFC).

4. Taxable-plastic bag.

5. Herbicide which is restricted from use.

6. Pesticide which is restricted from use.

7. Forest product preservative which is restricted from use.

8. Warehouse disinfectant which is restricted from use.

TAXPAYER

1. Environmental protection taxpayer is organizations, households and individuals producing, importing goods under taxable subject.

2. Environmental protection taxpayer in some specific cases shall be provided for as follows:

a) in case of goods importing commission, the person who entrusted importing goods shall be taxpayer;

b) In cases where organizations, households and individuals act procurement hub of coal to develop small, retail but they cannot produce the documents proving that goods have been paying environmental protection tax, the organizations, households individuals act as procurement hub shall be taxpayer.

TAX BASE

1. Tax base of environmental protection is the number of taxable goods and absolute rate.

2. The number of taxable goods shall be provided for as follows:

a) For goods produced in the country, the number of taxable goods is the quantity of goods produced and sold, exchanged, internally consumed, donated;

b) For imported goods, the number of taxable goods is the quantity of imported goods.

TAXABLE TIME

1. For goods manufactured, sold, exchanged, donated, taxable time is the time transferring the ownership or right to use goods.

2. For manufactured goods brought into internal consumption, taxable time is the time when taxable goods brought into use.

3. For imported goods, taxable time is the time of registration of customs declarations.

For gasoline, petroleum produced or imported for sale, taxable time is the time when the business hub of petrol and oil sold.

TAX DECLARATION, TAX CALCULATION AND TAX PAYMENT

1. The tax declaration, tax calculation, tax payment for environmental protection on goods produced and sold, exchanged, internally consumed, donated shall be made by the month and the provisions of the law on tax administration.

2. The tax declaration, tax calculation, tax payment for environmental protection on imported goods shall be made at the same to time of import tax declaration and tax payment.

3. Environmental protection tax is only paid once for goods produced or imported.

THE LAW ON EXPORT AND IMPORT DUTIES

GENERAL PROVISIONS

This Law provides for taxed goods, taxpayers, basis for tax calculation, time for tax calculation, tariff schedules, anti-dumping duty, countervailing duty, safeguard duty imposed upon exports and imports; tax exemption, tax reduction, refund of export and import duties.

TAXED GOODS

1. Goods exported and imported through a country's border and border checkpoints.

2. Goods exported from the domestic market into free trade zones; goods imported from free trade zones into the domestic market.

3. Goods indirectly exported-imported; goods exported and imported by enterprises exercising their right to export, import, or distribute.

4. The following goods do not incur export and import duties:

a) Goods in transit;

b) Goods that are humanitarian aid or grant aid;

c) Goods exported from a free trade zone to abroad; goods imported from abroad to a free trade zone and used within such free trade zone; goods transported from one free trade zone to another;

d) Amounts of petroleum used as severance tax paid to the State upon its exportation.

TAXPAYERS

1. Owners of exports and imports.

2. Entrusted exporters and importers.

3. People entering and leaving the home country carrying exports or imports, sending or receiving goods through the home country's border and border checkpoints.

4. Taxpayers' guarantors and other entities authorized to pay tax on behalf of taxpayers, including:

a) Customs brokerage agents in case authorized by the taxpayer to pay export and import duties;

b) Providers of postal services or international express mail services paying tax on behalf of taxpayers;

c) Credit institutions or other organizations operating under the Law on credit institutions that provide guarantee or pay tax on behalf of taxpayers;

d) People authorized by goods owners in case goods are gifts of individuals; any luggage sent before or after its owner's arrival or departure;

dd) Any branch of an enterprise authorized to pay tax on its behalf;

e) Other people authorized to pay tax on behalf of taxpayers as prescribed by law.

5. Any person who purchases or transports goods within the tax-free allowance applied to border residents which are sold domestically instead of being consumed or used for manufacture; foreign traders permitted to deal in exports and imports at bordering markets as prescribed by law.

6. Owners of exports or imports that are initially tax-free but then taxed.

7. Other cases prescribed by law.

TAXABLE VALUE AND TIME FOR TAX CALCULATION

1. The taxable value is the customs value prescribed by the Law on Customs.

2. The time for calculating export or import duty is the time of registration of the customs declaration.

In case of exports or imports that are not subject to taxation, exempt from export or import duties, or applying in-quota duty rates or fixed duty but then the eligibility for tax exemption or in-quota duties is changed as prescribed by law, the time for tax calculation is the time of registration of the new customs declaration.

The time of registration of the customs declaration shall comply with regulations of law on customs.

ANTI-DUMPING DUTIES

1. Conditions for applying anti-dumping duties:

a) The imports being dumped in the home country and the dumping margin must be determined;

b) The dumping causes or threatens to cause considerable damage to domestic manufacturing or prevents the formation of domestic manufacturing.

2. Rules for applying anti-dumping duties:

a) Anti-dumping duty may only be applied to a reasonable extent to prevent or minimize damage to domestic manufacturing;

b) The anti-dumping duties shall be applied after an investigation is carried out and conform to the investigation conclusion as prescribed by law;

c) Anti-dumping duty shall be imposed upon dumped imports in the home country;

d) The application of anti-dumping duties must not cause damage to domestic socio-economic interest.

COUNTERVAILING DUTIES

1. Conditions for applying countervailing duties:

a) It is determined that imports are subsidized as prescribed by law;

b) The imports cause or threaten to cause considerable damage to domestic manufacturing or prevent the formation of domestic manufacturing.

2. Rules for applying countervailing duties:

a) Countervailing duties may only be applied to a reasonable extent to prevent or minimize damage to domestic manufacturing;

b) The countervailing duties shall be applied after an investigation is carried out and conform to the investigation conclusion as prescribed by law;

TAX REDUCTION

1. Exports and imports that are damaged or lost under customs supervision and the damage or loss is verified by a competent organization, tax reduction shall be granted.

The level of reduction shall be proportional to the loss of goods. Tax is exempt if the exports or imports are completely damaged or lost.

2. The procedures for tax reduction shall comply with regulations of law on tax administration.

TAX REFUND

Cases of tax refund:

a) Any taxpayer who has paid export duty or import duty but has no exports or imports, or the quantity of exports or imports is smaller than the quantity on which duty is paid;

b) Any taxpayer who has paid export duty but the exports has to be re-imported shall receive a refund of export duty and does not have to pay import duty;

c) Any taxpayer who has paid import duty but the imports has to be re-exported shall receive a refund of import duty and does not have to pay export duty;

d) Any taxpayer who has paid tax on goods imported to serve manufacture or business operation and they have been used for manufacture of exports and the products are already exported;

dd) Any taxpayer who has paid tax on machinery, equipment, tools, vehicles of organizations and individuals that are permitted to be temporarily imported for re-export, except for those rented to execute investment projects, construction and installation, manufacture, when they are re-exported to abroad or exported to a free trade zone.

Conclusion

Thank you again for downloading this book on *"TAX LAW: Essential Legal Terms Explained You Need To Know About Tax Law!"* and reading all the way to the end. I'm extremely grateful.

If you know of anyone else who may benefit from the informative legal words presented in this book, please help me inform them of this book. I would greatly appreciate it.

Finally, if you enjoyed this book and feel that it has added value to your study or career in any way, please take a couple of minutes to share your thoughts and post a REVIEW on Amazon. Your feedback will help me to continue to write the kind of Kindle books that helps you get results. Furthermore, if you write a simple REVIEW with positive words for this book on Amazon, you can help hundreds or perhaps thousands of other readers who may want to enhance their legal vocabulary have a chance getting what they need. Like you, they worked hard for every penny they spend on books. With the information and recommendation you provide, they would be more likely to take action right away. We really look forward to reading your review.

Thanks again for your support and good luck!

If you enjoy my book, please write a POSITIVE REVIEW on amazon.

-- Dr. Peter Johnson --

Check Out Other Books

Go here to check out other related books that might interest you:

Legal Terminology And Phrases: Essential Legal Terms Explained You Need To Know About Crimes, Penalty And Criminal Procedure

http://www.amazon.com/dp/B01L5EB54Y

LAW ON INTELLECTUAL PROPERTY: Essential Legal Terms Explained You Need To Know About Trademarks, Copyrights, Patents, and Trade Secrets!

https://www.amazon.com/dp/B07PFP3MDY

COMPANY LAW: Mastering Essential Legal Terms Explained About Limited Liability Companies, Joint-Stock Companies, Partnership, Private Enterprises, And Groups of Companies!

https://www.amazon.com/dp/B07P2PRVMJ

INVESTMENT LAW: Essential Legal Terms Explained You Need To Know About Law On Investment!

https://www.amazon.com/dp/B07P79D925

LABOR LAW: Essential Legal Terms Explained You Need To Know About Law On Labor!

https://www.amazon.com/dp/B07PFD2CML

CIVIL LAW: Mastering Essential Legal Terms Explained About Civil Rights, Guardianship, Civil Transactions, Civil Obligations, Civil Liability, Civil Contracts And Civil Procedure!

https://www.amazon.com/dp/B07P5GS8LD

Legal Vocabulary In Use: Master 600+ Essential Legal Terms And Phrases Explained In 10 Minutes A Day

http://www.amazon.com/dp/B01L0FKXPU

Civil Law Vocabulary In Use: Master 350+ Essential Civil Law Terms And Phrases Explained With Examples In 10 Minutes A Day.

https://www.amazon.com/dp/B0781TQWGV

Criminal Law Vocabulary In Use: Master 400+ Essential Criminal Law Terms And Phrases Explained With Examples In 10 Minutes A Day.

https://www.amazon.com/dp/B078KLR51Z

Administrative And Tax Law In Use : Master 300+ Administrative And Tax Law Terms And Phrases Explained With Examples In 10 Minutes A Day.

https://www.amazon.com/dp/B07JMD546J

Productivity Secrets For Students: The Ultimate Guide To Improve Your Mental Concentration, Kill Procrastination, Boost Memory And Maximize Productivity In Study

http://www.amazon.com/dp/B01JS52UT6

Shortcut To Ielts Writing: The Ultimate Guide To Immediately Increase Your Ielts Writing Scores

http://www.amazon.com/dp/B01JV7EQGG

www.ingramcontent.com/pod-product-compliance
Lightning Source LLC
Chambersburg PA
CBHW030453220526
45464CB00006B/2522